AMAZING
JORDAN

ALL YOU NEED TO KNOW

Published by Promo Skills (New Edition)

Table Of Contents

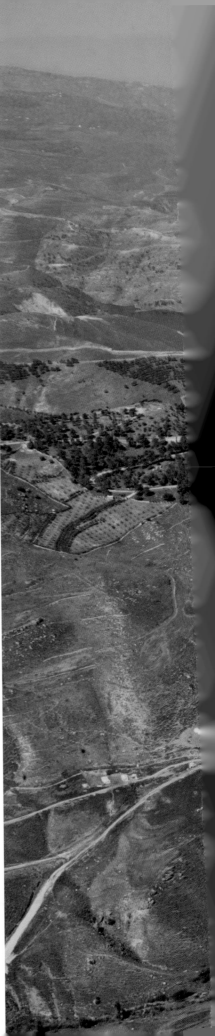

Welcome To Jordan

Welcome to Jordan! Jordan is a tourism treasure box, filled with opportunities. The more you learn about the different regions of the kingdom, the more you will want to explore.

Want to taste fine cuisine, enjoy Arab fusion music and shop in neighborhood shops? Come to Amman, where fabulous restaurants beckon, the arts scene is vibrant and funky markets are the new meeting places. Come wander through Jabal Amman or down town, and learn more about the history of this city, one of the oldest continually inhabited cities in the world. You might see ancient ruins from your window.

If you want to relax and unwind, the Dead Sea is the place for you, with its selection of hotels and spas at 405 meters below sea level. There is something magical about bobbing in the salty waters, knowing that it's impossible for you to sink. Or maybe it's that spa treatments that await you at the lowest point on earth.

If your tastes run more to water sports, Aqaba will meet your needs, with its coral reefs and excellent diving. Come find your wild side at one of the nature reserves run by the RSCN (The Royal Society for The Conservation of Nature) and Wild Jordan. Go for a day hike from the Ajloun reserve to Ajloun castle, or dine by candlelight at Wadi Feynan's eco-lodge. Watch the birds at Azraq reserve, the oryx at Shaumari or hike to Nabatean ruins in Wadi Dana. Maybe you'll spy some ibex at Wadi Mujib. Regardless of the adventure you choose, you'll have a great time!

Wander through the mists of time. Whether your tastes run to Roman ruins like Jerash, abandoned cities like Umm Al-Jimal, the Umayyad desert castles or the fortresses of Karak, Shobak and Ajloun, the past is very present in Jordan. Religious pilgrimage sites like Mount Nebo or the tomb of Zeid ibn al-Haritha, the Prophet's adopted son (PBUH), have drawn visitors for centuries.

Petra, just named one of the New Seven Wonders of the World, will take your breath away. With its Siq, carved by earthquakes out of solid rock, giving way to the first glimpse of the manmade Treasury, it is a sight not to be missed, either by day or Night. The rose-red city, and the spectacular views of Wadi Araba from the various high places, will haunt you until you return again and again.

Ride a camel in Wadi Rum, the Valley of the Moon. The silence of the desert will still your soul, and you'll come to a new appreciation for the people who traveled and lived here before cars and trucks. The beauty of the desert will amaze you, as will the surprises around every corner.

Meet the people. Jordanians are some of the most hospitable people on earth. Bargain in Al-Balad (down town), shop for rugs in Madaba, share a glass of tea with your guide in Wadi Rum. You won't forget the kindness you'll be shown.

Ahalan Wa-Sahalan. Welcome to Jordan. We're glad you're here.

The
Royal
Family

The Hashemites, Jordan's Royal Family can trace their ancestry directly back to the Prophet Mohammed (PBUH) through his daughter, Fatima, and her son, Hassan. Those who are descended from Hassan are known as Ashraf, the Arabic plural for honorable. For centuries, the Ashraf have been leaders in the Hijaz region, which includes what is now Jordan. The most prominent was Mohammed bin Aoun, who was Emir of Mecca in the 19th century.

In the recent history, Sharif Hussein bin Ali led the Great Arab Revolt of 1916-1917, waging guerilla warfare against the Ottoman Turks in order to gain independence for his people. His aim was to establish an independent and unified Arab state from Aleppo to Aden, which would embrace Islamic ideals and include ethnic and religious minorities.

His son, Emir Abdullah bin Hussein, established the Emirate of Transjordan in 1921. Under his rule, Jordan gained its independence on March 22, 1946, and King Abdullah was crowned two months later. Having led troops during the Revolt, King Abdullah was passionate about his country's freedom and about creating a progressive role for Jordan. Unfortunately, on July 20, 1951, King Abdullah was assassinated as he walked into the al-Aqsa Mosque for Friday prayers, accompanied by his grandson, Hussein, with whom he was very close.

King Talal bin Abdullah succeeded his father after his death. For reasons of ill health, King Talal abdicated in 1952 in favor of his son, Prince Hussein. As the prince had not yet attained his majority under the Islamic calendar, a regency council was formed until he reached eighteen.

King Hussein was crowned May 2, 1953. He became known as a passionate advocate for peace, not only working tirelessly to inspire Jordanians, but people the world over. His policies for developing Jordan's infrastructure led to increased stability in the kingdom and the creation of a larger class of professionals from all parts of Jordan. King Hussein succumbed to cancer on February 7, 1999, and was succeeded by his eldest son, King Abdullah II.

A thoroughly modern monarch, His Majesty King Abdullah II was born in Amman on January 30th, 1962, and was educated in Jordan, Britain and the United States. He served as an army officer for many years before assuming the throne. He also traveled on official missions and served as Regent in the absence of King Hussein from the country on many occasions. His Majesty strongly supports the creation of sustainable economic opportunities to improve the lives of all Jordanians. Under his leadership, Jordan has been admitted to the World Trade Organization and has put into place economic reform packages and ratified agreements to create Free Trade Areas with the United States, the European Union, and many Arab countries. King Abdullah II is married to Queen Rania, they have four children, two sons, Prince Hussein and Prince Hashem, and two daughters, Princess Iman and Princess Salma.

Our Country

Jordan is a land of history, with some of the oldest human civilizations leaving their mark. Today, one can still trace their movements in the castles and ruins that dot the landscape, and that tell the tale of how Jordan has been the meeting point for the Middle East and beyond for centuries.

Jordan comprises an area of 92,300 square kilometers, 91,971 of which are land and only 329 of which are water, with a coastline of only 26 kilometers. Most of the land is arid desert plateau. There is a highland area in the west and the Great Rift Valley separates the east and west banks of the Jordan River. The lowest point in Jordan and the World, is the Dead Sea, at 405 meters below sea level, and the highest point in Jordan is Jabal Rum, at 1,734 meters above sea level.

Jordan's population of over six million is generally homogenous. ethnic Jordanians include Circassians and Armenians. The median age of the population is 23.5 years, and is growing at 2.4%, due to births and immigration. 92% of Jordanians are Sunni Muslim, with 6% Christians. About 90% of the population is literate.

Recently, Jordan has begun to build up its tourist infrastructure, taking advantage of the enormous interest worldwide in eco-tourism. Jordan's location on the Great Rift Valley provides it with amazing geographical sites such as the Dead Sea and Wadi Dana, and it hosts a unique combination of flora and fauna, which it has made strides in protecting. Its amazing number of sites sacred to Muslims and Christians has made it a draw for religious travelers. Visitors interested in secular history can enjoy a variety of opportunities including Roman, Byzantine and Islamic sites, such as Qasayr Amra, now a UNESCO World Heritage Site.

Other unique destinations, such as Wadi Rum and Petra, have their own draw. The Royal Society for the Conservation of Nature, is leading the way in the kingdom with eco-tourism, opening several eco-lodges and reserves to bring attention to the exquisite beauty of Jordan's wild places.

Jordan is a special place, with outlets for every interest. Where else could you climb to the highest place in a country during the day and enjoy your dinner overlooking the lowest place on earth? Jordan's unique blend of the old and the new mystifies and delights, keeping visitors coming back for more.

Please enjoy getting to know the treasure box of riches that is Jordan.

Petra

Petra

In 2007, Petra was chosen as one of the "New Seven Wonders of the World" not just for the beauty of its rose-colored sandstone, or for its setting in the midst of about 100 ruggedly dramatic square kilometers of Wadi Araba, but because this area is a living museum of 10,000 years of human history. Petra's history tells the story of many civilizations. A cross roads for trade, Petra's architecture shows Assyrian, Greek, Roman, and Byzantine influences. In fact, the word "Petra" is derived from the Greek word for rock.

Excavations tell us that nearby Al-Beidha was a prosperous village 9,000 years ago, contemporaneous with Jericho. The next residents in the area were the Edomites, biblical mountain-dwellers who battled for their freedom from the Judeans. The Nabateans, who were mainly comprised of nomadic herders and raiders from Western Arabia, settled in the area in about the 4th century BC to make their living from levying taxes and protection fees on travelers. Their strong belief in solving conflicts through diplomacy rather than war probably contributed to the longevity of their culture. While there are historical records of discord with the Greeks, the Nabateans were primarily focused on furthering their trading goals. There is also evidence of Hellenistic influence in Petra from about 150 BC, which coincides with the spread of Nabatean trade routes into Syria. By the 4th century BC, Petra had centered its commercial base on trade in bitumen, frankincense, salt, and copper. Between the 1st centuries BC and AD, Petra gained a reputation for its progressive and effective systems of commerce and justice.

Ironically, given the effort that the Nabateans made to preserve their independence from Rome, most of the surviving records about Nabatean culture are from Strabo, a Roman scholar. According to his writings, while the Nabateans had a humane monarchy, they also enjoyed a system of democracy, and were concerned, almost to the point of obsession, with accumulating both material wealth and water, which accounts for the many systems

of cisterns and water harvesting still visible in modern Petra.

The Roman leader Pompey tried to annex Petra in 63 BC after he successfully conquered Syria and Palestine, but was bought off by the Nabatean leader Aretas III. The Romans eventually annexed Petra in 106 AD.

During the Byzantine period, a bishopric was created in Petra and some buildings were converted for Christian use. On the morning of May 19, 363 AD, a huge earthquake hit Petra and many of the free-standing buildings were destroyed. The region never entirely recovered from this, although Petra continued to be inhabited for centuries. While the Crusaders built a town at Wu'eira, it was abandoned 60 years later. However, when J. L. Burckhardt, a Swiss explorer traveling under the name Ibrahim ibn Abdullah, entered Petra in 1812, he did so as the first Westerner in living memory.

Today, as in the Nabateans' time, visitors enter through the Siq, the great crack in the rock that leads into the heart of the area. Before the mouth of the Siq, visitors pass by the Djinn blocks, huge carved blocks of stone that may represent the Nabatean god Betyl. The name comes from the local Bedouin, who long ago believed that the blocks were inhabited by djinn, or spirits. Close by is the Obelisk Tomb, thought to have been built in the 1st century BC, with its crown of four obelisks. At the entrance to the Siq are six obelisk-shaped carvings and inscriptions, the most important of which tells the story of a resident of Requem, an archaic name for Petra, who had been returned to the area after dying in Jerash.

The Siq was carved, not by human hands, but by tectonic forces during a long-forgotten earthquake. Ranging from 50 meters wide to only about 5, the Siq follows a meandering, 1.25 kilometer path, bounded by walls about 100 meters tall. In the Siq, it is still possible to see sections of the paved Nabatean road, water channels, niches that previously held statues of various gods, and weathered carvings, as well as where the grain of the sandstone on one wall matches exactly the grain on the other wall. The narrowness of the Siq, and its tall stone walls, made it a safe entry for the camel trains carrying incense, cloth and spices from places like Oman, Syria and India. Trade and the accumulation of wealth were so important to the Nabateans that merchants who suffered a loss during a year were fined.

The Siq ends directly in front of the Treasury (Al-Khazneh), the most well known of Petra's monuments, which has been immortalized in countless photographs and in the film, "Indiana Jones and the Last Crusade". The building, 43 meters by 30 meters, was deeply carved out of the living rock. As is the case with much of Petra, there are more stories than facts regarding the Treasury. Although the story goes that a Pharaoh hid his fortune in the great urn at the top of the façade, thus providing the name, the building is actually believed to be the tomb of the Nabatean King Aretas III. The bullet holes that mar the urn bear testimony of the number of people who have searched for the riches. Iconoclasts defaced the figures on the façade, thought to be Victories, or possibly depictions of Nabatean goddesses, and now their true identities may never be known. The niches carved into the rock halfway up the edges of the façade leave scope for the imagination to wonder about their use. The sun plays with the color of the stone, making this a sight to enjoy at any time of day, and more than once during a visit.

Leading into the center of the city are over 40 rock-cut tombs and houses, known as the Street of Facades. Some of them are merely the tops of doorways, as the outer siq has slowly filled with sand over the intervening centuries. This is the easiest place to explore. Many tombs were destroyed when the Romans enlarged the Nabatean-built theatre to about 7000 seats sometime after 106 AD. As sections of the theatre were constructed, rather than carved, it was badly damaged in the earthquake of 363 AD. Eventually, some of the damaged pieces were recycled and used in constructions in other parts of Petra.

From the Outer Siq a steep path that runs up to the High Place of Sacrifice, one of the oldest standing cultic altars. The path winds past several unusual sites. The Lion Monument

is a fountain that once channeled water to the city center. The Garden Temple Complex boasts two free-standing colonnades outside a shrine. The Roman Soldier's Tomb still has three statues in military dress on the façade. Inside, the stone has weathered magnificently.

The High Place of Sacrifice, oral-Madbah, is located at the top of Jabal Madbah, 200 meters above the theatre. This site may have been inherited from their Edomite predecessors. The isolation of this site, with its magnificent views, would have made this a perfect place for religious ceremonies. The two obelisks are dedicated to the Nabatean gods Dushara and Al-'Uzza.

The Royal Tombs are carved into the face of Jabal al-Khubtha. The Urn Tomb, which carries both Nabatean and Roman architectural details, was redesigned as a Christian church around 447 AD. About 150 rolls of papyri from the 6th century AD were discovered in the church during an excavation. Next to this is the Silk Tomb, badly eroded but brilliantly colored. The Corinthian Tomb, possibly the resting place of the ruler who built the Treasury, boasts a replica of it on the upper story. The Palace Tomb was the most ambitious of the Royal Tombs; when the builders ran out of rock to carve, they built the top of the façade. It is one of the more recent constructions and also one of the most ornamental. The final tomb is the Sextius Florentinus Tomb, which dates from 130 AD, and was built for the Roman governor of Arabia, with its faint inscriptions and carvings around the entrance.

The Colonnaded Street is a remnant from the Romans, built in 106 AD over an existing Nabatean street. This area was once filled with market sand shops and there is evidence that this was a popular area well into the 6th century BC. Overlooking the area are a Byzantine church with mosaic floors and the Temple of the Winged Lions, which was sacred to Atargatis, the Nabatean fertility goddess who was Dushara's consort. The Nymphaeum, a public fountain dedicated to water nymphs, was at one end. At the other end was the Temenos Gate, built in the 2nd century AD, which led to the sacred precinct around the Qasr al-Bint.

This free-standing Nabatean building was one of the few left standing after the earthquakes of the 4th and 8th centuries. Enough still stands to demonstrate how impressive it must have been. There is evidence that the Romans set the Palace on fire, and the two earthquakes then wreaked their own havoc. While the name means "Castle of the Daughter," it is believed to actually have been built in 30 BC for Dushara, and was one of the most important temples. In fact, there is evidence that Dushara's name (He of Sharra) came from the Sharra Mountains, which the Palace faces.

Other structures here include the Great Temple and the Petra Church. The Great Temple was built as a Nabatean temple in the 1st century BC. Records show that it was used for different religious purposes until late in the Byzantine period. It was once an impressive structure, with white and red stucco inside. It housed a 600-seat theatre, a paved courtyard, and a triple colonnade. Adjacent to the Great Temple, archeologists have recently uncovered a garden that may have served as a public park. Complete with pools, bridges and shade trees, the area resembles gardens built by Herod the Great in Judea. Herod's mother was Nabatean and he spent much of his childhood in Petra.

The Petra Church was first built by the Nabateans, redesigned by the Romans, and then burned down. However, it has recently been restored and the mosaics are lovely. At the top of Al-Habis, behind the Great Temple, is a small Crusader fort, perhaps built as a lookout post for the larger castle at Wu'eira. On the same hill are the self-described Unfinished Tomb and the Columbarium, which was perhaps used to keep messengers

pigeons. Overlooking al-Habis is Umm al-Biyara. While its face is carved with Nabatean tombs, at the summit are the remains of an Edomite village of Sela, dating from the 7th century BC. For sheer exhilarations, there are two sites that cannot be matched in Petra. The Monastery (Al-Deir), is similar to the Treasury, but larger, measuring over 46 meters by 40 meters, and faces an enormous flat plain. Its name comes from the crosses etched onto the back wall of the large interior chamber. From the Monastery, it is possible to see the other boggling site, the shrine and 14th century mosque of Nebi (Prophet) Haroun, where Moses's brother Aaron is said to have died and been buried. J.L. Burckhardt told the local Bedouin, who were uncomfortable with him visiting Petra, that he had a vow to sacrifice a goat at this tomb, and it was only this story that persuaded them to lead him in. This is the highest site in Petra, at 1,350 meters.

Other sites in the area include the 12th century Crusader castle at Wu'eira, the Siq Al-Barid, which became a "bedroom community" of Petra, the Neolithic village of Beidha, the Roman fortress ruins of Udruh and Daajaniyya, and the renovated Ottoman era village of Taybeh.

This microcosm of human history can take the visitor on a trip through time, back as far as 10,000 years. Visitors can be dazzled not only by the historical grandeur, but also by the natural beauty of the effects of sun, wind and weather on colorful stone. What is even more stunning is that excavations continue in the area. Most of Petra still lies beneath the sand. Who knows what treasures will be uncovered in the future, to further grace one of the New Seven Wonders of the World.

Amman

The fabled seven hills of Amman have given way to about twenty, and the magic of the city has grown as well. It is one of the oldest continually inhabited cities in the world and has seen most of the many civilizations that have come through the area. While most visitors only see the modern Amman, one of the enchanting aspects of the city is how a visitor can turn a corner and find a Byzantine church ruin in a busy shopping district, or see the ruins of an Ammonite fortress tower from the windows of a hotel. Like its Jabals, or hills, the fortunes of Amman have risen, fallen, and risen again.

In about 1200 BC, Amman became the capital of the Iron Age Ammonites, referred to as "Rabbath Ammon". The Ammonites, thought to be the ancestors of Lot, fought many battles with other regional leaders, and finally were defeated after a 10th century siege. Assyrians, Babylonians and Persians ruled the area over a period of several centuries until, in the 4th century BC, Ptolemy II rebuilt the city, renaming it Philadelphia for a former Ptolemaic leader.

Philadelphia, along with much of the region, was absorbed by Emperor Pompey into the Roman Empire in 63 BC. The city became part of the Decapolis and a prosperous trading center. It became known for its enlightened cultural centers and beautiful architecture. The 1700 meter-long walls of the Citadel, originally built during the Bronze Ages, were strengthened under the Romans and the Temple of Hercules was built during the reign of Marcus Aurelius (161-180 AD).

The Amphitheatre, Odeon, Forum and Nymphaeum were built downtown. Seating 6000, the Amphitheatre was built in the 2nd century AD. The structure had three layers of seating, with the rulers nearest the stage, the military in the middle, and the hoi polloi near the top, closest to the statue of Athena which scholars believe graced the alcove at the top of the Amphitheatre. A local story says that an underground tunnel runs from the alcove to the top of the Citadel. Cultural events are now held here, making it a striking backdrop for theatre and symphony concerts. The Odeon is a smaller, more intimate theatre, seating about 600 people.

It had a roof and was used most frequently for musical performances. The Forum is the square between the two theatres, and was once one of the largest public squares in the Roman world. It was lined along three sides by columns and on the fourth by Amman Stream. The Nymphaeum was a two-story complex with fountains, mosaics and a swimming pool. It was dedicated to water nymphs.

Amman received a bishopric during the Byzantine period, and several churches were built. The ruins of three churches can be found on the Citadel, on Jabal Weibdeh, and hidden away in the commercial center of Sweifieh.

During the Islamic caliphate in Damascus, Philadelphia changed its name to Amman and continued to flourish. The Umayyad Palace on the Citadel dates from 720 AD. It was destroyed by an earthquake in 749 AD and never rebuilt.

Amman's fortunes began to decline when the Abbasids moved the capital from Damascus to Baghdad. As Karak came to prominence during the Crusades, Amman's importance continued to slide, until it was primarily a place of exile. In 1806, Amman was reported to be uninhabited. However, in 1878, Circassian refugees began to arrive and settled in Al-Balad, what is now downtown. By 1900, there were 2000 inhabitants. To fill a need, merchants began to move in to the area from Salt, Syria, and Palestine.

By 1923, Al-Balad area had become crowded and many people were beginning to build their homes on top of Jabal Amman, which overlooks the area. This neighborhood is where King Hussein grew up, and was a nexus of influential families. By 1948, Amman's capital had risen to 25,000 inhabitants, but after the 1948 war, Jordan's population rose from 400,000 to about 1,300,000 in a year. From 1972-82, Amman grew from 21 square kilometers to 54 square kilometers. After 1991, and the return of 300,000 Palestinians and Jordanians after the 1991 Gulf War, the city grew again. The on-going Iraq War is the latest event to swell numbers in the city.

Today Amman is a city in sections. The working-class area of East Amman tends to be more conservative and more traditional. West Amman boasts villas and multi-story apartment complexes, modern shopping center and 5 stars hotels and restaurants. At times, walking through Amman can be like looking back wards through a tunnel, with so much history incorporated into so modern a city. But there is nothing more symbolic of Amman than sitting in one of the new cafes on Jabal Amman, listening to the call to prayer and looking out over to the Temple of Hercules on the Citadel.

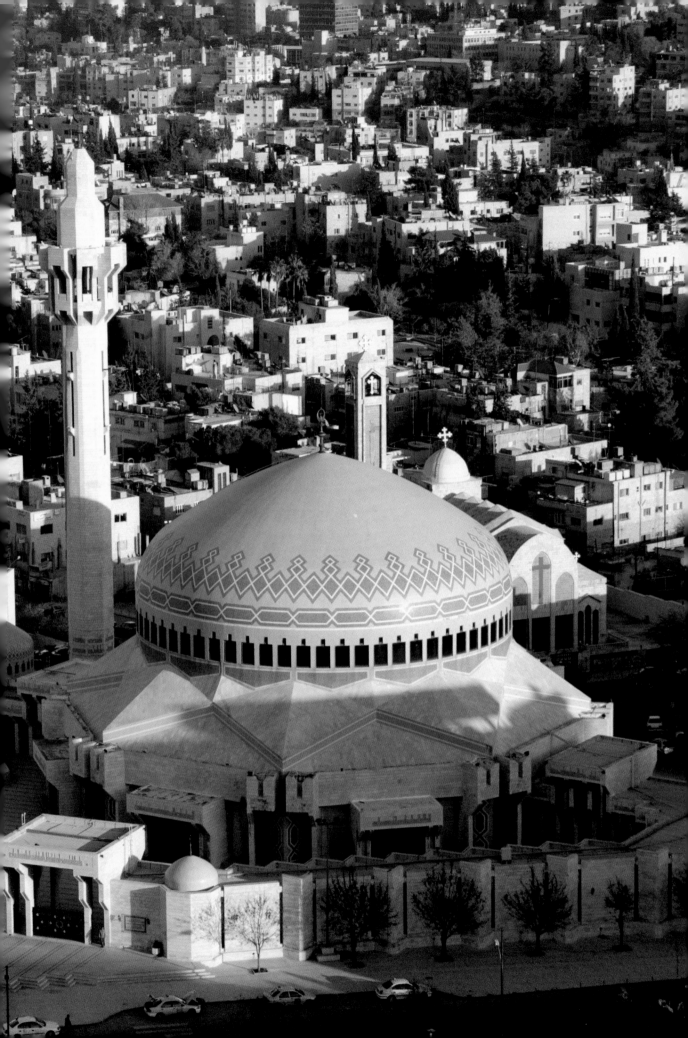

West
and
North

Salt

Filled with Ottoman-era houses, Salt is known as one of the most historic towns in Jordan. While the area has been settled since the Iron Age, it enjoyed its greatest period of prosperity during the end of the 19th century and the beginning of the 20th. Many of the families that influenced the creation of the modern state of Jordan come from Salt. As a consequence of not becoming the capital of the Emirate of Transjordan, Salt has been able to maintain its unique architectural legacy and small town charm.

The name Salt comes from either the Latin word "saltus" meaning forest, or from the word "sultana," as the area has been known for the quality of its grapes for centuries. There are Roman tombs on the outskirts of the city, and it was known as Saltus Hieraticon during Byzantine times.

In 1220 AD, the stronghold of the Mamluk Sultan Al-Malik Al-Mu'az was built on the crest of one of the steep hills in the town. Destroyed during the Mongol invasion of 1260, it was rebuilt by the Mamluks the following year.

Despite all of this upheaval, Salt has always been the division between the desert and the more agricultural valley region. Mentions of Salt, and its commercial importance, show up in writings from the Arab traveler Abu Al-Fida in the 13th century. 400 years later, the Swiss explorer Burckhardt noted that there were 400 Muslim and 80 Christian families living peacefully together in Salt. In 1806, Salt was said to be exempt from all taxes, and was an enormous trade center, even featuring cotton from Manchester, England, in its shops.

In the mid 19th century, Salt became an important administrative capital for the Ottomans and people migrated from Jerusalem, Nablus, Nazareth to live and prosper there. They celebrated their fortunes by building exquisite homes, some with domed and frescoed ceilings.

For the visitor, Salt is an opportunity to see the lovely facades of an Arab town during the time of the Ottoman Empire. Walking around Salt is a treat. From the Cultural Center to the Latin Monastery, from the houses to the shops, it is like taking a trip in a time machine. Salt's grace provides the visitor an enjoyable afternoon.

Jerash

Jerash is one of the best-preserved Roman-era cities in the world. Located only 40 kilometers north of Amman, visitors today can trace the chariot ruts on the Cardo, admire the mosaics which were laid contemporaneously to those found in Madaba, and test the acoustics of the North and South Theatres.

The history of Jerash can be traced in its name. The indigenous Semitic inhabitants in the 1st century BC called it "Garshu." The Greeks founded "Antioch on the Chrysorhoas," or the Golden River, on the same spot, naming it for the stream that runs through the area. The Romans who came in with Pompey changed the original name Garshu to "Gerasha". In the 19th century, the Arabs arabaized the name to "Jerash."

Jerash was linked to the trade routes by a series of roads that led to other major trade centers like Amman, Bosra, Damascus, Pella and Petra. Emperor Hadrian visited Jerash in 129 AD and a Triumphal Arch was built in his honor near the Hippodrome. Today, the Arch still stands and is in the final stages of restoration.

Jerash began to decline in the 3rd century AD. Uprisings, like the destruction of Palmyra in 273 AD, made caravans more dangerous and drove trade towards shipping, de-emphasizing the old trade routes. When Emperor Constantine converted the Byzantine to Christianity, a number of churches were built, many of them using stone recycled from the earlier temples. The Persians sacked Jerash in 614 AD, along with Damascus and Jerusalem, and the area was also impacted by the Muslim victory of 636 AD. Not long after, in 747 AD, the area was devastated by a series of major earthquakes. Its population shrank, and by the time the Crusaders came through, they described it as uninhabited.

The area was "rediscovered" by a German tourist, Ulrich Jasper Seetzen, who recognized the site and publicized it. Teams of archeologists from around the world have flocked to Jerash, and they continue to uncover new treasures. Not all the site has been worked yet, and more wonders may be discovered soon.

Visitors to Jerash today have a number of opportunities awaiting them. Chariot races are held in the Hippodrome, which was built between the 1st and 3rd centuries AD.

A walking tour through the site begins at the South Gate, built in 130 AD. The Oval Plaza, also known as the Forum, was an unusual construction in the classical world, as it is not symmetrical. Its shape gracefully joins the Temple of Zeus to the Cardo, leading attention away from the fact that they are not aligned properly. The Plaza is also unique in that it still has a collection of 1st century Ionic columns, while the columns that radiate out from it are Corinthian columns from the 2nd century. Some of the columns are a different color between the lower and upper halves, indicating how deeply the column was buried in sand.

The 1st century AD Temple of Zeus overlooks the Plaza. It was built on the remains of earlier sacred sites. Enormous blocks now filling the ruin were knocked down during an earthquake.

The nearby South Theatre is the largest at the site, able to hold at least 3000 people. It is in amazing condition, and the numbers are visible on many of the seats. The acoustics are fantastic, and the construction minimizes the amount of sun that may fall on spectators. The Theatre is in use today for concerts and other cultural events.

The Cardo, or the Street of Columns, links the Temple of Zeus with the Temple of Artemis. Some of its columns were deliberately built at different heights to show off the facades of the buildings behind them. Here are the visible wheel ruts from Roman chariots, testimony to the importance of this street.

The Cardo passes by the remains of the three Byzantine churches, Sts. Cosmas and Damian, St. John, and St. George. Most of the walls of the Byzantine churches at Jerash were leveled during earthquakes, but what makes them special are the mosaics. St.George, which is the furthest from the Temple of Artemis, is in the best shape, and there is evidence that it was used after the earthquakes of the 7th and 8th centuries. The other two were leveled. However, their destruction saved their mosaics from Christian iconoclasts, who disfigured the flooring of St.George's.

The Temple of Artemis is larger than the Temple of Zeus, as befitted the patron of Jerash and a goddess revered by the inhabitants of the Decapolis. This is thought to have been one of the most outstanding temples in any provincial Roman city. Built between 150 and 170 AD, the temple had twelve columns, which are still standing.

The nearby North Theatre was completed during the later half of the 2nd century. Greek inscriptions on some of the seats lead some experts to believe that this was a meeting place for regional or municipal officials.

Jerash amazes visitors not only because of the size of the site, but also the details which have survived so much. The carved lions at the Nymphaeum, the ruts in the streets of the Cardo, and the seat numbers at the South Theatre make it easy to imagine what life would have been like during its heyday. History seems so close in the peace of places like Jerash.

base as he evicted the Crusaders from Jordan in 1189. Located on the summit of Mount Auf about 1200 meters above sea level the original castle had four towers protected by a moat about 16 meters wide. Its commanding position allows views over Wadi Kufranjah, Wadi Rajeb and Wadi Al-Yabes, as well as over the Jordan Valley and Lake Tiberias, providing an important defensive advantage. It served as a check to the Crusader Belvoir Fort in Israel and was part of the messenger system of beacons and carrier pigeons that carried news from Damascus to Cairo in only one day.

In 1260 the castle was destroyed by the Mongol invaders, but was almost immediately rebuilt. Later in 1837 and 1927 earthquakes damaged the castle, but it is currently being restored. It is one of the best examples of Arab military architecture in the Levant.

After walking across the bridge over the dry moat, walk through the doorway into the main body of the castle. Don't miss the carvings of the pairs of birds, indicating the importance of carrier pigeons to its history. The galleries and rooms form a warren to wander through, with fabulous glimpses of the surrounding countryside visible from every arrowslit. Architectural features such as the gap in the ceiling for pouring boiling oil, and the storehouses of stone catapult missles, allow the imagination free rein. It is worth climbing to the top of the castle for the views and an interesting perspective of the shape of the castle. RSCN has a guided hike here from the Ajloun Reserve, which provides not only an interesting walk through the region, but also a unique perspective on the castle's defenses.

Kaneesit Mar Elyass, or St. Elijah's Church, has been known as a sacred place for many years. Excavations carried out in the late 1990s uncovered a Byzantine cross-shaped building measuring 33 x 32 meters, with mosaic floors covered in geometric or floral designs. One mosaic states in red letters that the presbyter Saba and his wife offered the church as an expression of their faith in the year 622 AD; this is the same year that Prophet Mohammed (PBUH) went to Mecca. Another smaller room has a mosaic floor and cultural artifacts that date from the 2-3rd century.

RSCN's Ajloun Reserve is located on 13 acres of oak, pistachio and carob trees, with seasonally available tents, cabins and a center for education. Several hikes are available, including the guided hike to Mar Elyass and its continuation to Ajloun Castle. Another guided hike climbs up to the eagle habitat, down to the RSCN community-based soap factory in Ourjan, and then to a delicious lunch hosted in one of the local farms.

At its highest point, Ajloun sits 1500 meters above sea level; a quarter of an hour later, in the Jordan Valley, the land drops to 412 meters below. The drama of the area, its bio-diversity and the connection of the people to the area make this a memorable place to learn about the rich history Jordan has to offer.

Umm Qais

Sitting on a high promontory overlooking Lake Tiberias, the Jolan Heights and the Jordan Valley, Umm Qais is the most dramatically situated of Jordan's Roman era towns. It also is perhaps the most dramatic to look at, as its location in the northwest corner of the kingdom provided both white stone and black basalt as natural building materials. A former member of the Decapolis, its name in during the Roman era was Gadara, which means a stronghold. Umm Qais, its more recent name, and the name of the nearby village, is derived from the Arabic word for junction or border station. Both are apt, one for its strategic height and the other for its position on the trade routes, connected to sites everywhere.

Gadara was originally built by the Greeks in the 4th century BC. In 218 BC, it was besieged by Antiochus III, the Seleucid ruler, who forded the Jordan River and overran Pella on his way. When Pompey formed the Decapolis in 63 BC, Gadara saw an economic upturn and a building surge. Mark Antony sent Herod the Great to deal with the Nabateans, who at this time controlled the trade routes up to Damascus. This high-handed interference with local events did not sit well with the people of Gadara, and they protested vehemently. Gadara became known as an arts city, with writers, philosophers and playwrights flourishing there. Two of the most famous were Menippos, a former slave turned satirist, and Oinomaos, the philosopher. This may be the biblical location where Jesus cast devils into swine, which then drowned themselves in the waters of Lake Tiberias.

Many experts believe that a popular pastime was to take the baths at Al-Himma in the village of Mukheiba, and then to relax in Gadara. Many people from all over the Roman Empire visited the area, based on evidence unearthed during excavations. Strabo, the Roman historian, also discusses Gadara and the baths. This relaxing option is still possible today.

Gadara continued to grow and in the 7th century received a bishopric. However, after several destructive earthquakes, the site was deserted, until the Ottoman Turks substantially rebuilt it. The proximity of the Roman ruins to the Ottoman town is intriguing. Local legend has it that Umm Qais is where the first agreement with the British was signed in 1920, as they had the first Jordanian government.

Major sites to see include the original Roman amphitheatre and the archeological museum, which is housed in a restored home of an Ottoman governor, Bait Rousan.

Strolling along the colonnaded street, wandering in the basilica and viewing the nymphaeum are all pleasant, as are the baths, the 16th century octagonal church and the underground mausoleum. A memorable ending to a visit to Umm Qais and Al-Himma is a meal on the terrace of the guesthouse, enjoying the view and reminiscing about your day.

Umm Al-Jimal

The Nabateans were people of surprises. Not only did they create the amazing city of Petra, they built the northern city of Umm Al-Jimal. Using the local rough black basalt instead of the soft rose sandstone of Wadi Musa, they created an eerie black city whose name, "Mother of Camels," indicates its function as a trading town, as it had precisely what caravans needed: water, food, shelter, and people to buy things. Built only 6 kilometers from the Roman Via Nova Triana, which linked northern Jordan and the Decapolis with the south and trading points farther out, Umm Al-Jimal was well-placed to take advantage of the spice, incense, and silk routes.

Evidence points to Umm Al-Jimal being inhabited since the 1st century AD. The town seems to have gone through three stages: a small village in the 2nd and 3rd centuries, a protected Roman town from the 4th – 5th centuries, and a flourishing trading and agricultural city between the 5th and 8th centuries. The earthquake of 747 AD leveled many buildings, and the city was not really inhabited after that, aside from serving as a base for Druze refugees in the early 19th century and for French troops during WWI. Sometime in the 3rd century, the town faced some kind of a threat, for they reinforced their defensive wall with tombstones. Like Nabatean sites elsewhere in Jordan, the inhabitants of Umm Al-Jimal were canny about water harvesting. There are several large cisterns still evident, which would have allowed for water needs and for irrigation.

The Nabatean inhabitants of Umm al-Jimal did not take the time with the stone here as they did in Petra. While their architecture was clever, there is little decoration. Walls, doors, even ceilings were made from the locally available basalt. They used a technique called corbelling, placing large stones over intersecting stones to cover

a large roof area. The fact that they used almost no wood is probably why so much at the site is still standing. The Romans, and those who followed, followed similar building plans but there is no sign of any attempt to control or plan building in the town. One of its charms is how everything is all together.

There are many things to see in Umm Al-Jimal. There are the ruins of a Nabatean temple, several churches, and the great barracks just at the entrance. The Gate of Commodus was built during the reign of Marcus Aurelius and his son, Commodus. The best way to enjoy the site is to wander and imagine.

The cleverness of the Nabateans, who seemed to make communities everywhere they went, is clearly underscored here in Umm Al-Jimal. Their ability to catch and retain water made this lonely outpost into a trade city. While quite different from the planned city of Petra, Umm Al-Jimal has an eerie charm which haunts visitors until they return.

The Baptism Site

The third most holy site for Christians in the world, after the Church of the Holy Sepulcher and the Church of the Nativity, is the site of the baptism of Jesus Christ, known in Arabic as al-Maghtas. Excavations at Wadi Kharrar carried out after the 1994 peace treaty found evidence of a complex of churches, hermit cells and other buildings described in the writings of many pilgrims who have visited the site since the 2nd century AD. Now preserved as a tourist destination, al-Maghtas attracts tourists year-round.

The holiness of this site for Christians inspired the Byzantines to build a monastery in the 5th and 6th centuries AD. This complex contained several churches, barracks for the monks, a caravenserai for pilgrims and an impressive water system. Al-Maghtas was part of the pilgrim trail that included Mt. Nebo and Jerusalem. The geometric shapes and crosses decorating the mosaic illustrate the iconoclasm of the early Christian church, which believed that figures should not be portrayed in art. The Western Church contained a rock-cut apse that extended under one of the pools. The oldest building, believed to be the Prayer Hall, may date from the beginning of the Byzantine era.

Tudius, a pilgrim to al-Maghtas in 530 AD, described the baptism site as five miles from the Dead Sea, and talked about the unique Church of Bethany, which was built on platforms in the early 6th century to prevent flood damage. He also mentioned a small hill on the site, identifying it as the place where Prophet Ilyas was lifted bodily to heaven in a whirlwind. The most famous pilgrim in recent times, Pope John Paul II, called for blessings upon the Kingdom of Jordan, His Majesty the King, and all the people of Jordan, Christians and Muslims together, during his visit.

Today al-Maghtas is a beautiful site, full of peace. Along with other religious sites, such as Mukawir, Lot's Cave and Mount Nebo, al-Maghtas attracts pilgrims from all over the world, just as it has for centuries.

The
South

Madaba

The fertility of Madaba's plains have made it a strategic location for 3500 years. Fought over by many people during different times, it later became a Nabatean town. During the Byzantine era, the city became a bishopric and the mosaics, for which it became famous, were laid. Today, the city is still famous for mosaics, both historical and for its mosaic school, the only one of its kind in the Middle East.

Many biblical civilizations coveted the rich plains surrounding Madaba. In 106 AD, the Romans became the governors, and Madaba gained a colonnaded street and the usual impressive public buildings of a provincial town. The town failed, however, after the earthquake of 747 AD, and lay abandoned for about 1100 years.

In the 1880s, local fighting in Karak drove 2000 Christians to settle in Madaba. As they began to dig foundations for their houses, they began to uncover mosaics. From then on, Madaba has been a heaven for archeologists and a nightmare for construction workers.

In or around 562 AD, many exquisite mosaic floors were laid in Madaba, including the Chapel of St. Theodore, now part of the Madaba Cathedral. In the Church of the Apostles, a mosaicist named Salamanios completed a masterwork. The oldest and most famous floor, the Mosaic Map, was discovered in 1884 in the Greek Orthodox Church of St. George. It was originally laid in 560 AD. Centering on Jerusalem, the map portrays the region with accuracy and humor. Archeologists have been able to positively identify most of the 150 named sites due to the accurate portrayals of natural features such as the River Jordan or the Dead Sea, as well as the labels. Only one-third of the map has survived.

The Archeological Park is located on the foundations of the Church of the Virgin Mary, and its floor is part of the collection. A mosaic found at Herod's castle in Mukawir is said to be the oldest mosaic found in Jordan, dating from the 1st century BC. The charming Hall of Seasons was found under a Madaba house. Across the preserved Roman road, complete with wheel ruts, are the foundations of the Church of the Prophet Elias, constructed in 608 AD.

Other tourist opportunities abound. The Burnt Palace is a 6th century luxury palace destroyed about 749 AD by fire and earth tremors, but which still boasts mosaic floors, mostly depicting animals and hunts. The Madaba Museum contains jewelry and ethnic costumes, as well as more mosaics. The unique Madaba Mosaic School seeks to preserve the craft and to teach conservation techniques.

A number of historical sites surround Madaba. Mt. Nebo is owned by the Franciscan fathers and has been part of the traditional Christian pilgrimage path for centuries. The traditional path included Jerusalem, Mt. Nebo, and a bath at Hammamat Ma'in, where Herod is said to have bathed. The new hotel and spa here makes this pilgrimage end in comfort and luxury.

Madaba is an unusual place. Once a Roman town, it is hard to find evidence of that now, but the Byzantine influence defines the tourism aspect of the area. The mosaics that were laid here long ago, and the ones being created now, set Madaba apart.

Karak

The enormous Crusader castle of Karak looms about 1000 meters above the Dead Sea Valley, a strategic link in the vital communication and protection system of castles that spread from Aqaba to Turkey. Karak was on the trading route between Egypt and Syria during biblical times, and later civilizations also recognized the advantages of the location. The castle has known happiness, but it has also known cruelty. Modern visitors will enjoy the spectacular views and the sandwiched layers of history.

During biblical times, Karak, known then as Kir, Kir Moab and Kir Heres, was the capital of Moab. The city can be found on the famous mosaic map in Madaba. Later used by the Greeks and Romans, its name was changed to Characmoba.

In the twelfth century, the Crusader king Baldwin I of Jerusalem commissioned Payen the Cupbearer to build the fortress of Karak. It became the capital of the Crusader Oultrejouirdain district, and became rich levying taxes on traders, travelers and agricultural produce. Karak is halfway between Shobak and Jerusalem, and its success helped Jerusalem prosper.

In the late 13th century, the Mamluk Sultan Beibars renovated the castle, deepened the moat and built the lower courtyard. Although damaged by an earthquake in 1293, the Ottomans also used the castle, after local fighting in the1880s forced the Christian inhabitants of Karak to flee to Madaba and Ma'an. Peace was restored only after a significant number of troops were stationed in the town.

Crossing over the wooden bridge over the dry moat, visitors enter through the Ottoman's Gate. To the left is the Crusader's Gallery, or the stables, at the end of which is a headless stone carving. Some claim it is Saladin, but as it dates from the 2nd century AD, it is likely a Nabatean carving. To the right are passages containing the kitchens and dining areas, as well as barracks. Coming out into the light, the favorite, dizzying drop of de Chatillon is on the left. Ahead is another set of passages, containing a mosque, a church, a prison and a marketplace. In the distance, Umm al-Thallaga is visible (the Mother of Snow), the mountain that was the biggest defensive threat to Karak. Here, at the Mamluk keep built in 1260, the defenses were strongest. Down below is the Mamluk courtyard and towers overlooking Wadi Karak, possibly down to the sites of Sodom and Gomorrah.

While the castle is being restored, and much of it is open to visitors, there are still some passages that are off-limits. It is tempting to imagine what treasures lie within. With any luck, Karak will give up more secrets to us in the near future.

Shobak

P art of the great beacon chain of Crusader fortresses, Shobak Castle is by far the most lonely. Built in 1115 AD by Baldwin I, who later built Karak, it was originally known as Mont Realis (Montreal) and was the first outpost of the kingdom of Jerusalem in the Crusader district of Outrejordain. Situated on an isolated knoll overlooking the trade routes that ran through the wadi below, Shobak is breathtaking.

The original entrance to Shobak Castle was through a dog-legged triple gate. Above this is the Crusader Church, with strategic views of the old village. There are several wells found within the castle walls, although the main water source was the spring at the foot of the hill. One of the treasures of this site is secret passage of over 350 steps that goes down to the spring, ensuring that during times of siege, the castle would have access to adequate supplies of fresh water. Baldwin I's court, a large room with antechambers running around it, has been partially reconstructed. Other rooms hold olive presses and a second church. It is still possible to see the cisterns, baths and pipes for harvesting rainwater.

Shobak fell to Saladin in 1189. In the 14th century the Mamluks took the castle and renovated it. Many of the outer walls now feature beautiful Kufic and Quranic inscriptions. The Mamluks built a watchtower and used the court as a school.

Shobak's daunting position made it a strong sentinel during the 12th century. The visible bones of the castle provide a startling insight into its anatomy, both as a Crusader castle and as a Mamluk edifice. Today, it is wonderful, romantic destination. The tranquility of the site, and its magnificent views, allow for peaceful reflection.

Wadi Rum

Falling approximately 600 meters from the high plateau of Ras Al-Naqab, Wadi Rum stretches 2 kilometers by 130 kilometers. This series of valleys covered in softly colored sand, punctuated by huge, imposing, fantastically shaped jabals, is one of the most memorable destinations in Jordan, and has been so since the dawn of time. Deep in the valleys, far from any visible human habitation, it is possible to believe the view has not changed much since the beginnings of human habitation in the Valley of the Moon, approximately 800 BC. T.E. Lawrence, the legendary Lawrence of Arabia, came here many times, both in his pursuit of success during the Great Arab Revolt of 1917-1918, but also because he found solace in the isolation of Wadi Rum.

Rum still rewards visitors today with peace and unceasing beauty. The magnificence of Rum lies primarily in its amazing geology.

Underneath the floors of the wadis, which lie between 900-1000 meters above sea level, is pre-Cambrian granite, created two billion years ago. In the sandstone strata of the jabals, it is possible to read the geologic history of the area. Red is Cambrian, pale grey is Ordovician, and whitish is Silurian. Separating them are layers of quartz, shale and conglomerates. The weather has shaped them, creating formations like birthday cakes, mushrooms, melting wax,

archways and even one that looks like a giant face in profile. The springs that appear throughout Wadi Rum were created when ancient rainfall permeated the sandstone, was stopped by the granite, and found tiny fissures to form pools.

Paleolithic man lived in Wadi Rum, taking advantage of the abundant wildlife and the plentiful springs. Eventually, their life of constant wandering gave way to the Neolithic lifestyle, which introduced agriculture and animal husbandry. The Nabateans made Wadi Rum one of their major settlements outside of Petra. They built three dams in the area, and the remains of their aqueducts are still visible in certain locations. Other visitors to the area left their marks in messages scrawled on the rocks, ranging from Nabatean script to Minaean commentary. The Thamuds, a tribe from what is today Saudi Arabia, left the largest number of inscriptions, from signatures to religious exhortations to messages of love.

The first mention of Wadi Rum was possibly as "Aramaua" in Ptolemeus' Geography. It is referred to as "Ad" in the Qur'an, according to some scholars. Wadi Rum was popular with travelers because of its abundance of food and water, making travel and trading easier, as well as its proximity to Petra, by far the largest urban center in the region.

While wildlife populations have decreased over the years, patient visitors can still find animals and birds, such as the hyrax, fennec foxes, gerbils and the Arabian sand cat. Ibex and gazelle herds still exist, it is possible to hear the musical howls of wolves. Vultures and eagles, as well as the smaller Sinai rosefinches and crested larks, populate the area, as well as the ubiquitous snakes, scorpions, and camel spiders.

Hiking and camping opportunities dot the region. The visitor's center near Rum Village is a good place to start a visit. Hot air ballooning is one of the most dramatic ways to see Wadi Rum, but guided jeep tours are also possible. The most traditional way to experience Wadi Rum, however, is by camel. The stillness, broken only by the wind, the groans of the camels and the sibilant commands of the guides, is phenomenal, with visits to the Burdah Rock Bridge, the five kilometer long Barrah Siq, the Red Sands or the Seven Pillars of Wisdom easy to arrange. T. E. Lawrence described Rum as "landscapes in childhood's dreams were so vast and silent," in The Seven Pillars of Wisdom.

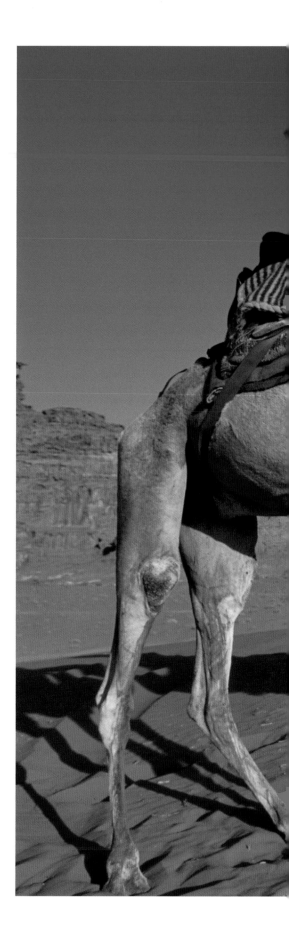

Aqaba

The seaside town of Aqaba is located on the Red Sea, within sight of Saudi Arabia and Egypt. Jordan may have only 26 kilometers of coastline, but they are being put to good use, and below the sparkling Red Sea waters are some of the most fantastic dive sites in the world. This area has been of strategic interest since old times, and evidence of these civilizations is still visible, although visitors may have to tear themselves away from the five-star hotels and the beach in order to do so. Aqaba is also popular as a base camp for travelers wanting to see Wadi Rum and Petra.

Near the road to Aqaba's airport is a Chalcolithic site, Tell Maquss. Dating back to 3500 BC, it was during this period that copper was firsts melted. The site is full of brick furnaces and slag heaps. Interestingly, the copper was brought from elsewhere, possibly from King Solomon's mines at Ezion Geber, just north of modern Aqaba. There is evidence here of trade with Somalia, Saba (Yemen) and Abyssinia (Ethiopia). Nearby, the ruined Edomite trading town of Tell al-Kheleifeh dates from the 1st century BC. The great trade route from Damascus snaked down through Amman and Petra, stopping at Aqaba before heading off to Palestine and Egypt.

Excavations have uncovered a town showing Nabatean, Roman and Byzantine influences, as each of these civilizations moved through the region between the 3rd century BC and the 4th century AD. A 3rd century AD building has been found which may be one of the oldest churches in the world.

Ayla became Aqaba under Mamluk rule and the Mamluk fort was built in the 14 century by Qansah Ghouri, one of the last sultans. The Ottomans did little to exploit Aqaba, and it diminished in importance over 400 years. Taken by force by Lawrence and the Arab forces during the Great Arab Revolt, it became a strategic port, allowing arms shipments and other supplies to come into Jordan from Egypt. The Hashemite coat of arms was added to the Mamluk fort after it was taken.

Today, Aqaba is a vibrant town that invites visitors, to enjoy the sun, sand, and fun. With approximately 335 days of sunshine per year and an average water temperature of 23 degrees Celsius, it is almost always a good day to be outdoors.

The Red Sea is one of the most diverse ecosystems in the world, offering some of the most colorful sea life anywhere. With over 500 species of coral, including the black archelia, which was first discovered by His Majesty, the late King Hussein, and over 1200 species of fish, Aqaba's 30 dive sites offer opportunities for everyone, from novices to experienced divers.

When visitors come up out of the water, they have their choice of leading hotels to enjoy, many with swimming pools and private beaches. There are opportunities for adventure on dry land as well, such as wandering around the ruins of Ayla, which was visited by Chinese, Moroccan, Syrian and Egyptian traders. Close to the Mamluk fort is a museum, housed in the former home of Sharif Hussein bin Ali. Petra, is two hours away and Wadi Rum is only one hour, making travel simple.

Sun, fun, and history await visitors to Aqaba. Long a cross roads between Africa, Europe, and Asia, today the beach still lures visitors and adventures still start here. Some of the most beautiful sea life in the world swims beneath the waters of the Red Sea, and Aqaba has facilities to help visitors explore this realm, whatever their ability level. With the sun, the beach, the history and all the treats offered at the fine hotels, visitors might never want to leave!

Nature
Reserves

Jordan is blessed with an incredible natural diversity. Nowhere is this more visible than in the seven nature reserves of (RSCN) The Royal Society for the Conservation of Nature. From the desert oasis of the Azraq Wetland Reserve to the dramatic gorges and rivers of the Wadi Mujib Reserve, this system of reserves protects much of Jordan's most dramatic topography, in addition to the Kingdom's flora and fauna. The RSCN also protects the peoples of the reserve areas by creating sustainable economic options for them, either in the reserves or through its tourism arm, Wild Jordan.

The Dana Reserve is possibly the best known of Jordan's nature reserves. This showplace, set up in 1993, has become an exemplar of how to set up a sustainable, eco-friendly reserve. With its network of guided and unguided hiking trails, its campground, guesthouse and eco-lodge with their staffs of residents, its dramatic wadis and mountains dropping about 1600 meters from the highest

point, there are 320 square kilometers full of things to do and marvel at Most surprising is not the Nabatean tomb, but the sea urchin fossils, now so far from the sea!

Some of the animals in Dana are truly unique. The Caracal cat is such a great jumper that it can catch birds in midair. 80% of the world's population of Tristan's Serin, a small finch found only in the Middle East, lives in Dana. It is not uncommon for visitors to be serenaded at night by grey wolves, as at least three packs live within Dana.

Wadi Feynan is at the western edge of the Dana Reserve area. The primary destination here is the Feynan Eco-lodge, an adobe guesthouse powered entirely by solar energy and lit at night primarily by candles. It is located close to the ruins of Khirbet Feynan, the ruins of a community centered around a copper mine. There is evidence of inhabitants in this area during the Neolithic, Iron Age, Roman, Byzantine, and Early Islamic times.

The Desert
Castles

The Desert Castles

The eastern desert of Jordan is a bleak, forbidding place, filled with basalt, sand, and sky. During Roman times, Septimius Severus and Diocletian built a network of forts here, called the limes arabicus, to protect the eastern border of their new province. While many fell into disrepair, some were later restored by the Umayyads, and added to, to create their own settlements in the desert. Each building seems to have had its own role, whether as a hunting lodge, caravanserai, or meeting hall, designed to maintain ties with the local Bedouin. A Hungarian Arabist, Alois Musil, "rediscovered" Qasayr Amra and Qasr Tuba in 1898. Although the ruins of several are open to the public, three of them, Qasr Kharana, Qasayr Amra, and Qasr Azraq are special, due to the restoration of the site or because of their history.

The Ummayad Castles are a wonderful reason to visit the eastern desert. Whether used for defense or relaxation, they give a glimpse into a world few were privileged to see. The tall walls of Kharana, the frescoes of Amra, and the historical associations of Azraq make this journey rich and rewarding.

The last thirty years, Jordan has seen an emergence of modern indigenous art. Traditional arts have bloomed alongside more modern ideas, and a fusion of the two is reinvigorating the area's aesthetic sensibilities. This is apparent in both the independent and institutionalized arts scenes. In recognition of this, UNESCO named Amman as its Arab Culture Capital for 2002.

In 1979, the Royal Society of Fine Arts began to establish the collection that now fills the Jordan National Gallery of Fine Art. The aim of the Gallery is to promote and disseminate the arts of Islamic countries and the developing world.

Amman's arts scene is experiencing something of a renaissance. Musical groups that fuse East and West and the National Gallery, which provides an internationally recognized outlet for artists from the Arab and developing world, bring a diversity of viewpoints to the country, adding to the rich tradition of art in the region.

For further information, please visit:
www.jordanbooks.info